EXPLORING OUR OCEANS

PACIFIC OCEAN

by Avery Toolen

Ideas for Parents and Teachers

Pogo Books let children practice reading informational text while introducing them to nonfiction features such as headings, labels, sidebars, maps, and diagrams, as well as a table of contents, glossary, and index.

Carefully leveled text with a strong photo match offers early fluent readers the support they need to succeed.

Before Reading

- "Walk" through the book and point out the various nonfiction features. Ask the student what purpose each feature serves.
- Look at the glossary together. Read and discuss the words.

Read the Book

- Have the child read the book independently.
- Invite him or her to list questions that arise from reading.

After Reading

- Discuss the child's questions. Talk about how he or she might find answers to those questions.
- Prompt the child to think more. Ask: How do you think pollution harms ocean wildlife?

Pogo Books are published by Jump!
5357 Penn Avenue South
Minneapolis, MN 55419
www.jumplibrary.com

Library of Congress Cataloging-in-Publication Data

Names: Toolen, Avery, author.
Title: Pacific Ocean / by Avery Toolen.
Description: Minneapolis: Jump!, Inc., 2023.
Series: Exploring our oceans | Includes index.
Audience: Ages 7-10
Identifiers: LCCN 2021053976 (print)
LCCN 2021053977 (ebook)
ISBN 9781636907772 (hardcover)
ISBN 9781636907789 (paperback)
ISBN 9781636907796 (ebook)
Subjects: LCSH: Pacific Ocean–Juvenile literature.
Marine ecology–Pacific Ocean–Juvenile literature.
Classification: LCC GC771 .T66 2023 (print)
LCC GC771 (ebook) | DDC 551.46/14–dc23
LC record available at
https://lccn.loc.gov/2021053976
LC ebook record available at
https://lccn.loc.gov/2021053977

Editor: Jenna Gleisner
Designer: Emma Bersie

Photo Credits: MogensTrolle/iStock, cover; Edwin Verin/Shutterstock, 1; Brian Lasenby/Shutterstock, 3; Harvepino/Shutterstock, 4; Alberto Loyo/Shutterstock, 5; Keystone/Getty, 6 (top); Rich Carey/Shutterstock, 6-7; KEVIN ELSBY/Alamy, 8-9; Rod Haestier/Alamy, 10-11; Andrew Sutton/Shutterstock, 12; Martin Voeller/Shutterstock, 13; Richard Whitcombe/Shutterstock, 14-15 (top); AshtonEa/Shutterstock, 14-15 (bottom); Anton Balazh/Shutterstock, 16; Kirk Wester/Shutterstock, 17; Jeff Milisen/Alamy, 18-19; Mark Kiver/Alamy, 20-21; blue-sea.cz/Shutterstock, 23.

Printed in the United States of America at Corporate Graphics in North Mankato, Minnesota.

TABLE OF CONTENTS

CHAPTER 1

DEEP OCEAN

Which of Earth's five oceans is the biggest? It is the Pacific Ocean!

Because this ocean is so big, its temperature changes depending on the location. The western part is warm. It can be more than 82 degrees Fahrenheit (28 degrees Celsius). The northern part is cold. It can get below freezing. Ice floats in the water.

Trieste

The Pacific Ocean is the deepest ocean. The deepest point is in the Mariana **Trench**. It is called Challenger Deep. The ocean floor is 36,201 feet (11,034 meters) deep. That is almost seven miles (11 kilometers)! In 1960, the *Trieste* reached it.

TAKE A LOOK!

Challenger Deep is deeper than Mount Everest is tall. Take a look!

The Ring of Fire is a chain of **volcanoes**, volcanic islands, underwater mountains, and trenches. It is nearly 25,000 miles (40,200 km) long! It stretches across the Pacific from Asia to North and South America.

TAKE A LOOK!

Where is the Pacific Ocean and the Ring of Fire? Take a look!

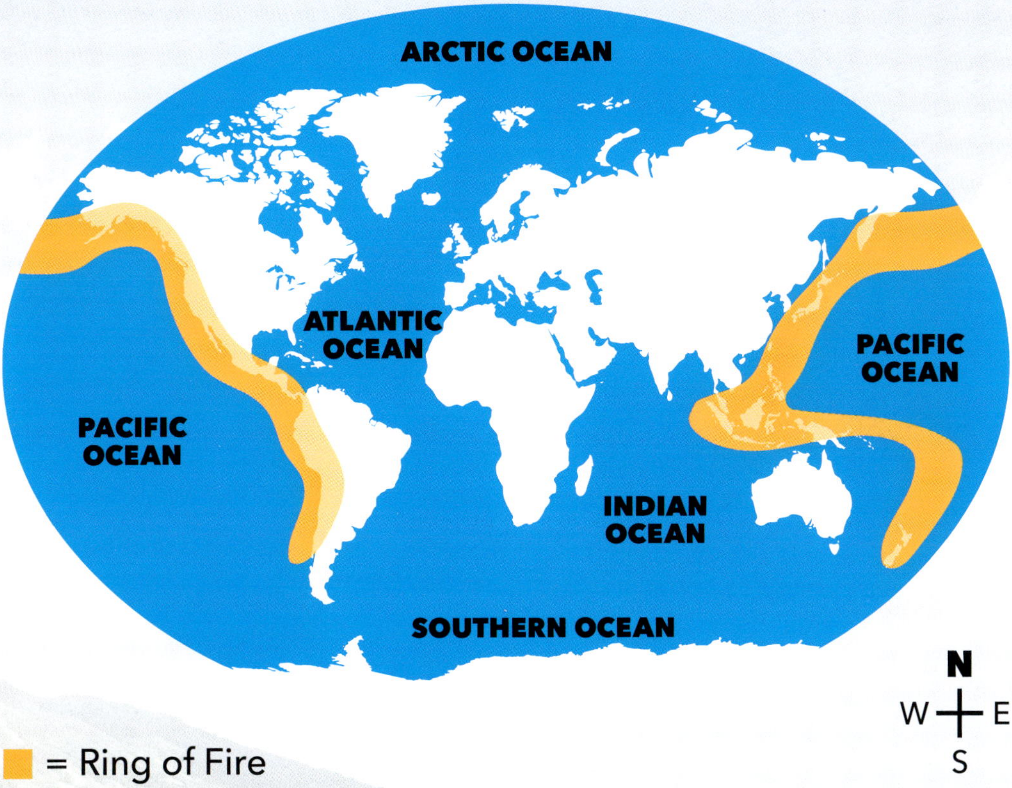

Earthquakes happen in the Ring of Fire. They cause tsunamis. These big waves cause damage and flooding onshore.

DID YOU KNOW?

Hurricanes happen in the Pacific Ocean. They are also called typhoons and tropical cyclones. The name depends on where the storm starts.

CHAPTER 2

PACIFIC WILDLIFE

Many kinds of whales and dolphins swim in the Pacific Ocean. Blue whales can grow 100 feet (30 m) long!

The giant Pacific octopus lives in the northern Pacific. It changes color to blend in.

coral reef

kelp bed

Coral reefs are in warm, **shallow** waters. Fish, sea snakes, and sea turtles live in them.

Kelp beds are on the rocky shores of North and South America. They are usually in cold water. Fish, brittle stars, and sea urchins live in them. Sea otters, sharks, and whales hunt.

CHAPTER 3

THE OCEAN AND US

People began exploring this ocean more than 3,000 years ago. Polynesians rowed canoes across it from the western and southern Pacific. Some made it to Hawaii.

Today, ships carry goods across the Pacific. Los Angeles, California, is a busy **port**.

garbage

Climate change is warming Earth's oceans. Scientists study its effects.

Pollution is also a problem. The Great Pacific Garbage Patch is an area where it collects. It makes up an area bigger than Texas. Animals eat the garbage. It can harm them.

DID YOU KNOW?

We can all help keep the oceans clean. How? **Recycle**. Use less plastic. Pick up litter.

People visit **shipwrecks**. Many are in the Graveyard of the Pacific. This is an area off the coast of Washington and Oregon. A **sandbar** is just under the water. Ships hit it. Some wrecks have washed up onshore.

Would you like to explore the Pacific Ocean? What would you like to see?

shipwreck

ACTIVITIES & TOOLS

TRY THIS!

FOOD OR PLASTIC?

Many ocean animals have a hard time telling the difference between food and pieces of plastic that end up in the ocean. See what they experience in this activity.

What You Need:

- packing peanuts or small pieces of Styrofoam
- popcorn
- cardboard box or other container
- watch or timer

1. **Put an equal amount of packing peanuts or small pieces of Styrofoam and popcorn in a box or container. Mix them up.**
2. **Have a friend or adult set a timer for 30 seconds.**
3. **When he or she says go, pick out all the pieces of popcorn you can. These represent the food an ocean animal might eat. The packing peanuts or Styrofoam represent garbage.**
4. **When your time is up, think about the activity. Was it hard to pick out the pieces of popcorn? Why do you think this is?**

GLOSSARY

climate change: Changes in Earth's weather and climate over time.

coral reefs: Long lines of coral that lie in warm, shallow waters.

earthquakes: Sudden, violent shakings of the earth that may cause damage.

hurricanes: Strong storms with heavy rain and high winds.

kelp: A type of large brown seaweed.

pollution: Harmful materials that damage or contaminate the water, air, and soil.

port: A harbor or place where ships can dock or anchor safely to load and unload cargo.

recycle: To process old items such as glass, plastic, newspapers, and aluminum so they can be used to make new products.

sandbar: A ridge of sand in a river, bay, or along an ocean's shore.

shallow: Not deep.

shipwrecks: The remains of ships that have sunk at sea.

trench: A long, narrow hole in the ocean floor.

volcanoes: Mountains with openings through which molten lava, ash, and hot gases can erupt.

INDEX

TO LEARN MORE

Finding more information is as easy as 1, 2, 3.

1. Go to www.factsurfer.com
2. Enter "PacificOcean" into the search box.
3. Choose your book to see a list of websites.

FACT SURFER